ESTD          2017

# KIDS LIGHTHOUSE

ALL FOR HIS GLORY

To:_____
_____

From:_____
_____

A Father's Love

DEEP IN THE FOREST LIVED A
BABY PANDA BEAR
WHO ASKED...

# HOW MUCH DOES GOD LOVE ME?

THE BIG PANDA BEAR
REPLIED...

HAVE YOU EVER WONDERED
HOW BIG THE UNIVERSE IS?
HOW BIG AND HOW WIDE?

# DID YOU KNOW THAT GOD'S LOVE FOR YOU IS BIGGER THAN THE UNIVERSE?!

AND I PRAY THAT YOU, BEING ROOTED AND ESTABLISHED IN LOVE, MAY HAVE POWER, TOGETHER WITH ALL THE LORD'S HOLY PEOPLE, TO GRASP HOW WIDE AND LONG AND HIGH AND DEEP IS THE LOVE OF CHRIST, AND TO KNOW THIS LOVE THAT SURPASSES KNOWLEDGE—THAT YOU MAY BE FILLED TO THE MEASURE OF ALL THE FULLNESS OF GOD.

EPHESIANS 3:17-19

DEEP IN THE THE ARCTIC LIVED
A BABY POLAR BEAR
WHO ASKED...

CAN YOU COUNT HOW MANY
HAIRS ARE ON MY HEAD?

THE BIG POLAR BEAR
REPLIED...

# I CAN'T, BUT GOD CAN.

AND EVEN THE VERY HAIRS OF YOUR HEAD ARE
ALL NUMBERED.

MATTHEW 10:30

CURIOUSLY STANDING ON THE
SANDY SHORES WAS A BABY
SEAL WHO ASKED...

DOES GOD THINK ABOUT ME?

# THE BIG SEAL REPLIED...

# DID YOU KNOW THAT IF YOU WERE TO COUNT ALL OF GOD'S THOUGHTS FOR YOU, IT WOULD BE MORE THAN THE GRAINS OF SAND?!

HOW PRECIOUS TO ME ARE YOUR THOUGHTS, GOD!
HOW VAST IS THE SUM OF THEM!
WERE I TO COUNT THEM,
THEY WOULD OUTNUMBER THE GRAINS OF SAND

PSALM 139:17-18

RELAXING IN THE MOUNTAINS
WAS A BABY MOUNTAIN LION
WHO ASKED...

# DOES GOD KNOW ANYTHING ABOUT ME?

THE BIG MOUNTAIN LION
REPLIED...

# GOD KNEW EVERYTHING ABOUT YOU BEFORE YOU WERE EVEN BORN!

YOUR EYES SAW MY UNFORMED BODY;
ALL THE DAYS ORDAINED FOR ME WERE
WRITTEN IN YOUR BOOK
BEFORE ONE OF THEM CAME TO BE.

PSALM 139:16

PLAYING IN THE OCEAN WAS A
BABY DOLPHIN WHO ASKED...

IF I'M LOST AT SEA, WILL GOD STILL FIND ME?

THE BIG DOLPHIN REPLIED...

# GOD WILL ALWAYS KNOW WHERE YOU ARE!

WHERE CAN I GO FROM YOUR SPIRIT?
WHERE CAN I FLEE FROM YOUR PRESENCE?
IF I GO UP TO THE HEAVENS, YOU ARE THERE;
IF I MAKE MY BED IN THE DEPTHS, YOU ARE THERE.
IF I RISE ON THE WINGS OF THE DAWN,
IF I SETTLE ON THE FAR SIDE OF THE SEA,
EVEN THERE YOUR HAND WILL GUIDE ME,
YOUR RIGHT HAND WILL HOLD ME FAST.

PSALM 139:7-10

STANDING ON A MOUNTAINTOP
WAS A BABY BALD EAGLE
WHO ASKED...

DOES GOD ALWAYS WATCH

OVER ME?

THE BIG BALD EAGLE REPLIED...

# GOD ALWAYS WATCHES OVER YOU.

NOTHING IN ALL CREATION IS HIDDEN FROM GOD'S SIGHT.

HEBREWS 4:13

HOPPING IN THE OUTBACK WAS
A BABY KANGAROO WHO
ASKED...

HOW DID I GET IN YOUR TUMMY
BEFORE I WAS BORN?

THE BIG KANGAROO REPLIED...

# GOD PUT YOU THERE OF COURSE!

FOR YOU CREATED MY INMOST BEING;
YOU KNIT ME TOGETHER IN MY MOTHER'S
WOMB.
I PRAISE YOU BECAUSE I AM FEARFULLY AND
WONDERFULLY MADE;
YOUR WORKS ARE WONDERFUL,
I KNOW THAT FULL WELL.

PSALM 139:13-14

DEEP IN THE RAINFOREST
LIVED A BABY GORILLA WHO
ASKED...

# WHEN IT'S DARK, CAN GOD STILL SEE ME?

THE BIG GORILLA REPLIED...

# GOD CAN ALWAYS SEE YOU. DARKNESS IS JUST AS BRIGHT AS LIGHT TO GOD!

IF I SAY, "SURELY THE DARKNESS WILL HIDE ME
AND THE LIGHT BECOME NIGHT AROUND ME,"
EVEN THE DARKNESS WILL NOT BE DARK TO YOU;
THE NIGHT WILL SHINE LIKE THE DAY,
FOR DARKNESS IS AS LIGHT TO YOU.

PSALM 139:11-12

ACROSS THE TREES THERE
LIVED A BABY CHIPMUNK
WHO ASKED...

# WHERE CAN I RUN WHEN I'M SCARED?

THE BIG CHIPMUNK REPLIED...

# INTO GOD'S ARMS OF COURSE!

YOU ARE MY HIDING PLACE;
YOU WILL PROTECT ME FROM TROUBLE
AND SURROUND ME WITH SONGS OF
DELIVERANCE.

PSALM 32:7

AS ALL THE BABY ANIMALS STARED AT THE SAME BEAUTIFUL NIGHT SKY, THEY ALL ASKED THIS SAME QUESTION...

WILL I GET TO BE WITH GOD
ONE DAY?

ALL THE BIG ANIMALS
REPLIED...

JESUS TOLD US THAT HE IS GOING TO PREPARE A PLACE FOR US, AND ONE DAY, WE ALL GET TO BE WITH HIM, TOGETHER.

MY FATHER'S HOUSE HAS MANY ROOMS; IF THAT WERE NOT SO, WOULD I HAVE TOLD YOU THAT I AM GOING THERE TO PREPARE A PLACE FOR YOU? AND IF I GO AND PREPARE A PLACE FOR YOU, I WILL COME BACK AND TAKE YOU TO BE WITH ME THAT YOU ALSO MAY BE WHERE I AM. YOU KNOW THE WAY TO THE PLACE WHERE I AM GOING."

JOHN 14:2-4

THEN, ALL THE BABY
ANIMALS ASKED...

# HOW DO WE GET THERE?

AGAIN, ALL THE BIG ANIMALS
REPLIED THE SAME THING...

# THERE IS ONLY ONE WAY TO GET THERE, WE FOLLOW JESUS CHRIST. HE IS THE ONLY WAY.

THOMAS SAID TO HIM, "LORD, WE DON'T KNOW WHERE YOU ARE GOING, SO HOW CAN WE KNOW THE WAY?"
JESUS ANSWERED, "I AM THE WAY AND THE TRUTH AND THE LIFE. NO ONE COMES TO THE FATHER EXCEPT THROUGH ME.

JOHN 14:5-6

AGAIN, ALL THE BABY
ANIMALS ASKED...

WHAT ARE WE SUPPOSED TO
DO WHILE WE WAIT?

ALL THE BIG ANIMALS REPLIED
THE SAME WORDS...

GO INTO ALL THE WORLD AND PREACH THE GOSPEL
TO EVERY CREATURE.

MARK 16:15

God loves you more than you could ever imagine. He protects you, loves you, and takes care of you. He thinks about you and wants the best for you.

REMEMBER, WHILE WE WAIT FOR JESUS, WE ARE GIVEN THE INSTRUCTIONS TO TELL OTHERS ABOUT HIM.

THIS IS CALLED

The GReat CommissioN

# THERE IS NOTHING
# GREATER THAN
*A Father's Love*

To see more books by
Kids Lighthouse, please visit
KidsLighthouse.com

www.ingramcontent.com/pod-product-compliance
Lightning Source LLC
Chambersburg PA
CBRC090826120626
46547CB00008B/618